MW00417096

151
THINGS
GOD
CAN'T
DO

151
THINGS
GOD
CAN'T
DO

—— ✳ ——

MAISIE SPARKS

NEW YORK BOSTON NASHVILLE

Copyright © 2015 by Maisie Sparks

All rights reserved. In accordance with the U.S. Copyright Act of 1976, the scanning, uploading, and electronic sharing of any part of this book without the permission of the publisher is unlawful piracy and theft of the author's intellectual property. If you would like to use material from the book (other than for review purposes), prior written permission must be obtained by contacting the publisher at permissions@hbgusa.com. Thank you for your support of the author's rights.

Unless otherwise indicated, all Scripture quotations are taken from the King James Version (KJV) of the Holy Bible.

Scripture quotations marked NKJV are from the New King James Version. Copyright © 1982 by Thomas Nelson, Inc. Used by permission. All rights reserved.

FaithWords
Hachette Book Group
1290 Avenue of the Americas
New York, NY 10104
www.faithwords.com

Printed in the United States of America

WOR

First Edition: October 2015

10 9 8 7 6 5 4 3 2 1

FaithWords is a division of Hachette Book Group, Inc.
The FaithWords name and logo are trademarks of Hachette Book Group, Inc.

The Hachette Speakers Bureau provides a wide range of authors for speaking events. To find out more, go to www.hachettespeakersbureau.com or call (866) 376-6591.

The publisher is not responsible for websites (or their content) that are not owned by the publisher.

Library of Congress Cataloging-in-Publication Data has been applied for.

ISBN 978-1-4555-8923-4

151
THINGS
GOD
CAN'T
DO

1

—— ✽ ——

God can't love
you more.

Greater love hath no man than this, that
a man lay down his life for his friends.

John 15:13

2

---✦---

God can't love
you less.

And the son said to him, "Father, I have sinned against heaven and in your sight, and am no longer worthy to be called your son." But the father said to his servants, "Bring out the best robe and put it on him, and put a ring on his hand and sandals on his feet."

Luke 15:21–22 NKJV

3

---- ❊ ----

God can't lie.

That by two immutable things, in which it was impossible for God to lie, we might have a strong consolation, who have fled for refuge to lay hold upon the hope set before us.

Hebrews 6:18

4

✳

God can't leave you.

And, behold, I am with thee, and will keep thee in all places whither thou goest, and will bring thee again into this land; for I will not leave thee, until I have done that which I have spoken to thee of.

Genesis 28:15

5

✳

God can't be indifferent to your feelings.

For we have not an high priest which cannot be touched with the feeling of our infirmities; but was in all points tempted like as we are, yet without sin. Let us therefore come boldly unto the throne of grace, that we may obtain mercy, and find grace to help in time of need.

Hebrews 4:15–16

6

✿

God can't be far from those who draw near to Him.

Draw nigh to God, and he will draw nigh to you.

James 4:8

7

---
*

God can't be limited.

For with God nothing shall be impossible.

Luke 1:37

8

— ✽ —

God can't forsake you.

And be content with such things as ye have: for he hath said, I will never leave thee, nor forsake thee.

Hebrews 13:5

9

❋

God can't stop
loving you.

I have loved thee with an everlasting
love: therefore with lovingkindness have
I drawn thee.

Jeremiah 31:3

10

--- ✳ ---

God can't steal.

The earth is the LORD's, and the fulness thereof; the world, and they that dwell therein.

Psalm 24:1

11

✻

God's goodness and mercy can't ever stop following you.

Surely goodness and mercy shall follow me all the days of my life: and I will dwell in the house of the LORD for ever.

Psalm 23:6

12

❋

God can't be tempted with evil.

Let no man say when he is tempted, I am tempted of God: for God cannot be tempted with evil, neither tempteth he any man.

James 1:13

13

*

God can't be defeated.

O sing unto the LORD a new song; for he hath done marvellous things: his right hand, and his holy arm, hath gotten him the victory.

Psalm 98:1

14

✳

God can't forget about you.

Can a woman forget her sucking child, that she should not have compassion on the son of her womb? Yea, they may forget, yet will I not forget thee.

Isaiah 49:15

15

✳

God can't give you a spirit of fear.

For God hath not given us the spirit of fear; but of power, and of love, and of a sound mind.

II Timothy 1:7

16

God can't wait to answer your prayers.

It shall come to pass that before they call, I will answer; and while they are still speaking, I will hear.

Isaiah 65:24 NKJV

17

✤

God can't be prejudiced.

Of a truth I perceive that God is no respecter of persons: But in every nation he that feareth him, and worketh righteousness, is accepted with him.

Acts 10:34–35

18

✽

God can't leave the righteous in trouble.

Many are the afflictions of the righteous: but the LORD delivereth him out of them all.

Psalm 34:19

19

God can't allow His work to be done without Him.

I am the vine, ye are the branches: He that abideth in me, and I in him, the same bringeth forth much fruit: for without me ye can do nothing.

John 15:5

20

God can't let any evil plot against you succeed.

No weapon that is formed against thee shall prosper; and every tongue that shall rise against thee in judgment thou shalt condemn. This is the heritage of the servants of the Lord, and their righteousness is of me, saith the Lord.

Isaiah 54:17

21

✳

God can't change.

Jesus Christ the same yesterday, and
to day, and for ever.

Hebrews 13:8

22

✦

God can't remember sins that He's forgotten.

I, even I, am he that blotteth out thy transgressions for mine own sake, and will not remember thy sins.

Isaiah 43:25

23

❋

God can't produce bad fruit.

But the fruit of the Spirit is love, joy, peace, longsuffering, gentleness, goodness, faith, meekness, temperance: against such there is no law.

Galatians 5:22–23

24

❋

God's mercy can't end.

O give thanks unto the LORD, for he is
good: for his mercy endureth for ever.

Psalm 107:1

25

*

God can't ever lose His power.

And I heard as it were the voice of a great multitude, and as the voice of many waters, and as the voice of mighty thunderings, saying, Alleluia: for the Lord God omnipotent reigneth.

Revelation 19:6

26

❖

God can't leave you without a place to go.

The name of the LORD is a strong tower:
the righteous runneth into it, and is safe.

Proverbs 18:10

27

❉

God can't allow anything to separate you from His love.

For I am persuaded, that neither death, nor life, nor angels, nor principalities, nor powers, nor things present, nor things to come, nor height, nor depth, nor any other creature, shall be able to separate us from the love of God, which is in Christ Jesus our Lord.

Romans 8:38–39

28

❋

God can't be second in your life.

Thou shalt have no other gods before me.

Exodus 20:3

29

*

God can't swear
by anyone but Himself,
and He swore that
He would bless you.

For when God made promise to Abra-
ham, because he could swear by no
greater, he sware by himself, saying,
Surely blessing I will bless thee, and
multiplying I will multiply thee.

Hebrews 6:13–14

30

❋

God can't be
unforgiving to
those who ask for
forgiveness.

If we confess our sins, He is faithful and
just to forgive us our sins and to cleanse
us from all unrighteousness.

I John 1:9 NKJV

31

❊

God can't let anyone take you out of His hands.

And I give unto them eternal life; and they shall never perish, neither shall any man pluck them out of my hand.

John 10:28

32

✳

God can't wait for you to get right to take care of your wrongs.

But God commendeth his love toward us, in that, while we were yet sinners, Christ died for us.

Romans 5:8

33

❋

God can't be dethroned.

Your throne is established from of old;
you are from everlasting.

Psalm 93:2 NKJV

34

✳

God can't be unfaithful.

They are new every morning: great is thy faithfulness.

Lamentations 3:23

35

✳

God can't deny access
to those who come
through Jesus.

Jesus said to him, "I am the way, the
truth, and the life. No one comes to the
Father except through Me."

John 14:6 NKJV

36

✳

God can't let you down.

Now unto him that is able to keep you from falling, and to present you fault-less before the presence of his glory with exceeding joy, to the only wise God our Saviour, be glory and majesty, dominion and power, both now and ever. Amen.

Jude 1:24–25

37

❖

God can't accept divided loyalties.

No one can serve two masters; for either he will hate the one and love the other, or else he will be loyal to the one and despise the other. You cannot serve God and mammon.

Matthew 6:24 NKJV

38

❋

God can't leave you stranded.

What man of you, having an hundred sheep, if he lose one of them, doth not leave the ninety and nine in the wilderness, and go after that which is lost, until he find it? And when he hath found it, he layeth it on his shoulders, rejoicing.

Luke 15:4–5

39

✳

God can't sin.

Who did no sin, neither was guile found
in his mouth.

I Peter 2:22

40

*

God can't stop exceeding your expectations.

Now unto him that is able to do exceeding abundantly above all that we ask or think, according to the power that worketh in us.

Ephesians 3:20

41

* ✿ *

God's love can't be measured.

For God so loved the world, that he gave his only begotten Son, that whosoever believeth in him should not perish, but have everlasting life.

John 3:16

42

✻

God can't leave you the way He found you.

Therefore if any man be in Christ, he is a
new creature: old things are passed away;
behold, all things are become new.

II Corinthians 5:17

43

--- ❧ ---

God can't be pleased without faith.

But without faith it is impossible to please him: for he that cometh to God must believe that he is, and that he is a rewarder of them that diligently seek him.

Hebrews 11:6

44

✳

God can't remain in the grave; He lives forever.

I am he that liveth, and was dead; and, behold, I am alive for evermore.

Revelation 1:18

45

✻

God can't be fooled.

For the word of God is quick, and power-
ful, and sharper than any twoedged sword,
piercing even to the dividing asunder of
soul and spirit, and of the joints and mar-
row, and is a discerner of the thoughts and
intents of the heart.

Hebrews 4:12

46

✳

God can't cast out those who come to Him.

All that the Father giveth me shall come
to me; and him that cometh to me I will
in no wise cast out.

John 6:37

47

❋

God can't overlook genuine sacrifice.

And there came a certain poor widow, and she threw in two mites, which make a farthing. And he called unto him his disciples, and saith unto them, Verily I say unto you, that this poor widow hath cast more in, than all they which have cast into the treasury: For all they did cast in of their abundance; but she of her want did cast in all that she had, even all her living.

Mark 12:42–44

48

❊

God can't ask you
to do something
He can't do
through you.

For it is God which worketh in you both
to will and to do of his good pleasure.

Philippians 2:13

49

✦

God can't be
figured out.

As thou knowest not what is the way of
the spirit, nor how the bones do grow in
the womb of her that is with child: even
so thou knowest not the works of God
who maketh all.

Ecclesiastes 11:5

50

*

God can't know any other Gods.

Is there a God beside me? Yea, there is no
God; I know not any.

Isaiah 44:8

51

✳

God can't renege on His word.

God is not a man, that he should lie; neither the son of man, that he should repent: hath he said, and shall he not do it? Or hath he spoken, and shall he not make it good?

Numbers 23:19

52

❖

God can't enter your heart uninvited.

Behold, I stand at the door, and knock:
if any man hear my voice, and open the
door, I will come in to him, and will sup
with him, and he with me.

Revelation 3:20

53

❀

God can't leave His work undone.

It is finished.

John 19:30

54

❊

God can't deny you the chance to repent.

The Lord is not slack concerning his promise, as some men count slackness; but is longsuffering to us-ward, not willing that any should perish, but that all should come to repentance.

II Peter 3:9

55

✳

God can't ever
be out of control.

Jesus answered, Thou couldest have no
power at all against me, except it were
given thee from above.

John 19:11

56

❦

God can't allow His faithfulness to be refuted.

And ye know in all your hearts and in all your souls, that not one thing hath failed of all the good things which the Lord your God spake concerning you; all are come to pass unto you, and not one thing hath failed thereof.

Joshua 23:14

57

***

God can't despise
a contrite heart.

The sacrifices of God are a broken spirit:
a broken and a contrite heart, O God,
thou wilt not despise.

Psalm 51:17

58

❖

God can't be bought.

Again, the devil taketh him up into an exceeding high mountain, and sheweth him all the kingdoms of the world, and the glory of them; and saith unto him, All these things will I give thee, if thou wilt fall down and worship me. Then saith Jesus unto him, Get thee hence, Satan: for it is written, Thou shalt worship the Lord thy God, and him only shalt thou serve.

Matthew 4:8–10

59

❀

God's foundation can't be shaken.

Nevertheless the foundation of God standeth sure, having this seal, The Lord knoweth them that are his. And, let every one that nameth the name of Christ depart from iniquity.

II Timothy 2:19

60

✳

God can't allow Himself to be loved halfheartedly.

Jesus said unto him, Thou shalt love the Lord thy God with all thy heart, and with all thy soul, and with all thy mind.

Matthew 22:37

61

✳

God can't be impressed.

And all our righteousnesses are as filthy rags; and we all do fade as a leaf; and our iniquities, like the wind, have taken us away.

Isaiah 64:6

62

God can't go unnoticed.

The heavens declare the glory of God; and
the firmament sheweth his handywork.

Psalm 19:1

63

***

God can't withhold wisdom from those who seek it.

If any of you lack wisdom, let him ask of God, that giveth to all men liberally, and upbraideth not; and it shall be given him.

James 1:5

64

*

God can't make a succession plan.

I am Alpha and Omega, the beginning and the ending, saith the Lord, which is, and which was, and which is to come, the Almighty.

Revelation 1:8

65

※

God's kingdom can't be moved.

Wherefore we receiving a kingdom which cannot be moved, let us have grace, whereby we may serve God acceptably with reverence and godly fear.

Hebrews 12:28

66

God can't fail to care for you.

The LORD is my shepherd; I shall not want.

Psalm 23:1

67

God can't allow the order of His creation to cease.

While the earth remaineth, seedtime and harvest, and cold and heat, and summer and winter, and day and night shall not cease.

Genesis 8:22

68

✦

God can't deny Himself.

If we are faithless, He remains faithful;
He cannot deny Himself.

II Timothy 2:13 NKJV

69

*

God's grace can't be in short supply.

My grace is sufficient for thee: for my strength is made perfect in weakness.

II Corinthians 12:9

70

❋

God can't leave you without an escape plan.

There hath no temptation taken you but such as is common to man: but God is faithful, who will not suffer you to be tempted above that ye are able; but will with the temptation also make a way to escape, that ye may be able to bear it.

I Corinthians 10:13

71

❋

God can't let His anger linger.

For his anger endureth but a moment; in his favour is life: weeping may endure for a night, but joy cometh in the morning.

Psalm 30:5

72

*

God can't be shut out of anywhere.

Whither shall I go from thy spirit? Or whither shall I flee from thy presence? If I ascend up into heaven, thou art there: if I make my bed in hell, behold, thou art there. If I take the wings of the morning, and dwell in the uttermost parts of the sea, even there shall thy hand lead me, and thy right hand shall hold me.

Psalm 139:7–10

73

*

God can't be left without a witness.

Yet I have left me seven thousand in Israel, all the knees which have not bowed unto Baal, and every mouth which hath not kissed him.

I Kings 19:18

74

❋

God can't be unclear about His expectations of you.

And what doth the Lord require of thee,
but to do justly, and to love mercy, and to
walk humbly with thy God?

Micah 6:8

75

❧

God can't be outdone.

Among the gods there is none like unto thee, O Lord; neither are there any works like unto thy works.

Psalm 86:8

76

❋

God can't shortchange you.

And every one that hath forsaken houses, or brethren, or sisters, or father, or mother, or wife, or children, or lands, for my name's sake, shall receive an hundredfold, and shall inherit everlasting life.

Matthew 19:29

77

God can't allow His praise to be silenced.

Blessed be the King that cometh in the name of the Lord: peace in heaven, and glory in the highest. And some of the Pharisees from among the multitude said unto him, Master, rebuke thy disciples. And he answered and said unto them, I tell you that, if these should hold their peace, the stones would immediately cry out.

Luke 19:38–40

78

✳

God can't want for anything.

For every beast of the forest is mine, and the cattle upon a thousand hills. I know all the fowls of the mountains: and the wild beasts of the field are mine. If I were hungry, I would not tell thee: for the world is mine, and the fulness thereof.

Psalm 50:10–12

79

✻

God can't be outnumbered.

Fear not: for they that be with us are more than they that be with them.

II Kings 6:16

80

❋

God's plan can't be overruled.

The counsel of the LORD standeth for ever, the thoughts of his heart to all generations.

Psalm 33:11

81

❊

God can't neglect His children.

If ye then, being evil, know how to give good gifts unto your children, how much more shall your Father which is in heaven give good things to them that ask him?

Matthew 7:11

82

❊

God can't be unjust.

He is the Rock, his work is perfect: for all his ways are judgment: a God of truth and without iniquity, just and right is he.

Deuteronomy 32:4

83

*

God can't be too busy to take time for children.

But Jesus said, Suffer little children, and forbid them not, to come unto me: for of such is the kingdom of heaven.

Matthew 19:14

84

✳

God can't tolerate lukewarm believers.

I know thy works, that thou art neither cold nor hot: I would thou wert cold or hot. So then because thou art lukewarm, and neither cold nor hot, I will spue thee out of my mouth.

Revelation 3:15–16

85

✳

God can't forget those who serve Him.

For God is not unrighteous to forget your work and labour of love, which ye have shewed toward his name, in that ye have ministered to the saints, and do minister.

Hebrews 6:10

86

❋

God can't allow anything to escape His notice.

Are not two sparrows sold for a farthing? And one of them shall not fall on the ground without your Father. But the very hairs of your head are all numbered. Fear ye not therefore, ye are of more value than many sparrows.

Matthew 10:29–31

87

✳

God can't be given a job He can't handle.

Ah Lord God! Behold, thou hast made the heaven and the earth by thy great power and stretched out arm, and there is nothing too hard for thee.

Jeremiah 32:17

88

❋

God can't forsake
the righteous.

I have been young, and now am old; yet
have I not seen the righteous forsaken,
nor his seed begging bread.

Psalm 37:25

89

✻

God can't be happy about joyless givers.

Every man according as he purposeth in his heart, so let him give; not grudgingly, or of necessity: for God loveth a cheerful giver.

II Corinthians 9:7

90

✼

God's grace can't be measured.

And the grace of our Lord was exceedingly abundant, with faith and love which are in Christ Jesus.

I Timothy 1:14 NKJV

91

*

God can't let go of your hand.

Though he fall, he shall not be utterly cast down: for the LORD upholdeth him with his hand.

Psalm 37:24

92

❋

God can't refuse His support to the righteous.

Cast thy burden upon the LORD, and he shall sustain thee: he shall never suffer the righteous to be moved.

Psalm 55:22

93

✳

God can't be far from you in your time of need.

God is our refuge and strength, a very present help in trouble.

Psalm 46:1

94

✳

God can't fail to correct His children.

My son, despise not thou the chastening of the Lord, nor faint when thou art rebuked of him: For whom the Lord loveth he chasteneth, and scourgeth every son whom he receiveth.

Hebrews 12:5–6

95

❀

God can't disown you.

Fear not: for I have redeemed thee, I have called thee by thy name; thou art mine.

Isaiah 43:1

96

❦

God can't be uncaring.

Casting all your care upon Him, for He cares for you.

I Peter 5:7 NKJV

97

✳

God can't exhaust His mercy.

But the mercy of the LORD is from ever-lasting to everlasting upon them that fear him.

Psalm 103:17

98

*

God's love can't be self-centered.

Charity suffereth long, and is kind; charity envieth not; charity vaunteth not itself, is not puffed up, doth not behave itself unseemly, seeketh not her own, is not easily provoked, thinketh no evil; rejoiceth not in iniquity, but rejoiceth in the truth; beareth all things, believeth all things, hopeth all things, endureth all things.

I Corinthians 13:4–7

99

✽

God can't give anyone power over His life.

No man taketh it from me, but I lay it down of myself. I have power to lay it down, and I have power to take it again.

John 10:18

100

✳

God can't be equaled.

I, even I, am the LORD; and beside me there is no saviour.

Isaiah 43:11

101

❋

God can't see with human eyes.

For the LORD seeth not as man seeth; for man looketh on the outward appearance, but the LORD looketh on the heart.

I Samuel 16:7

102

✳

God can't deny your soul rest.

Come unto me, all ye that labour and are
heavy laden, and I will give you rest. Take
my yoke upon you, and learn of me; for I
am meek and lowly in heart: and ye shall
find rest unto your souls.

Matthew 11:28–29

103

*

God can't be beaten at giving.

For all things come of thee, and of thine own have we given thee.

I Chronicles 29:14

104

God's mercy can't be measured.

For as the heaven is high above the earth, so great is his mercy toward them that fear him.

Psalm 103:11

105

✳

God can't give
up on you.

Being confident of this very thing, that
he which hath begun a good work in
you will perform it until the day of Jesus
Christ.

Philippians 1:6

106

✦

God can't be unrighteous.

The LORD is righteous in all his ways,
and holy in all his works.

Psalm 145:17

107

※

God can't allow Himself to be manipulated.

Jesus said unto him, It is written again,
Thou shalt not tempt the Lord thy God.

Matthew 4:7

108

✳

God can't ignore great faith.

But he answered and said, It is not meet to take the children's bread, and to cast it to dogs. And she said, Truth, Lord: yet the dogs eat of the crumbs which fall from their masters' table. Then Jesus answered and said unto her, O woman, great is thy faith: be it unto thee even as thou wilt. And her daughter was made whole from that very hour.

Matthew 15:26–28

109

❋

God can't mislead you.

Trust in the Lord with all thine heart; and lean not unto thine own understanding. In all thy ways acknowledge him, and he shall direct thy paths.

Proverbs 3:5–6

110

✳

God can't stop being God.

From everlasting to everlasting, thou art God.

Psalm 90:2

111

---   ✳   ---

God can't act
with partiality.

There is neither Jew nor Greek, there is
neither bond nor free, there is neither
male nor female: for ye are all one in
Christ Jesus.

Galatians 3:28

112

✦

God can't be in the dark about anything.

Yea, the darkness hideth not from thee; but the night shineth as the day: the darkness and the light are both alike to thee.

Psalm 139:12

113

✢

God can't be
boxed in.

Behold, the heaven and heaven of heavens cannot contain thee; how much less this house that I have builded?

I Kings 8:27

114

✤

God can't be replaced in your life.

Then Simon Peter answered him, Lord, to whom shall we go? Thou hast the words of eternal life.

John 6:68

115

❋

God can't be told anything He doesn't already know.

I am God, and there is none like Me, declaring the end from the beginning, and from ancient times things that are not yet done.

Isaiah 46:9–10 NKJV

116

✻

God can't allow evil to have the last word.

But as for you, ye thought evil against me; but God meant it unto good, to bring to pass, as it is this day, to save much people alive.

Genesis 50:20

117

✳

God's salvation can't be earned.

For by grace are ye saved through faith; and that not of yourself: it is the gift of God: Not of works, lest any man should boast.

Ephesians 2:8–9

118

❋

God can't have anything dawn on Him.

Great is our Lord, and mighty in power;
His understanding is infinite.

Psalm 147:5 NKJV

119

✳

God can't stop thinking about you.

How precious also are thy thoughts unto me, O God! How great is the sum of them! If I should count them, they are more in number than the sand: when I awake, I am still with thee.

Psalm 139:17–18

120

❊

God can't tolerate evildoing.

For thou art not a God that hath pleasure in wickedness: neither shall evil dwell with thee. The foolish shall not stand in thy sight: thou hatest all workers of iniquity.

Psalm 5:4–5

121

❊

God's word can't be ineffective.

For he spake, and it was done; he commanded, and it stood fast.

Psalm 33:9

122

✳

God can't be deaf
to your cries.

The eyes of the LORD are upon the
righteous, and his ears are open unto
their cry.

Psalm 34:15

123

* * * ✳ * * *

God can't be boring.

In thy presence is fulness of joy; at thy right hand there are pleasures for evermore.

Psalm 16:11

124

---※---

God can't allow evil to go unpunished.

Vengeance is mine; I will repay, saith the Lord.

Romans 12:19

125

❋

God can't forgive you if you don't forgive others.

But if ye forgive not men their trespasses, neither will your Father forgive your trespasses.

Matthew 6:15

126

✳

God can't cease
to exist.

Before me there was no God formed,
neither shall there be after me.

Isaiah 43:10

127

＊

God can't disappoint those who wait on Him.

The LORD is good unto them that wait for him, to the soul that seeketh him.

Lamentations 3:25

128

---
*

God can't be blind to what you are doing.

The eyes of the LORD are in every place,
beholding the evil and the good.

Proverbs 15:3

129

❋

God can't exhaust His resources.

My God shall supply all your need according to his riches in glory by Christ Jesus.

Philippians 4:19

130

※

God can't desert the devout.

For the LORD loveth judgment, and forsaketh not his saints; they are preserved for ever: but the seed of the wicked shall be cut off.

Psalm 37:28

131

*

God can't be late.

Now Martha said to Jesus, "Lord, if You had been here, my brother would not have died...Jesus said to her, "Your brother will rise again."

John 11:21, 23 NKJV

132

❀

God's will can't be thwarted.

Whatsoever the Lord pleased, that did he in heaven, and in earth, in the seas, and all deep places.

Psalm 135:6

133

❋

God can't remain lost to those who search for Him.

And ye shall seek me, and find me, when
ye shall search for me with all your heart.

Jeremiah 29:13

134

❋

God can't leave you comfortless.

I will not leave you comfortless: I will come to you.

John 14:18

135

---

*

God can't let your enemies win.

And they shall fight against thee; but they shall not prevail against thee; for I am with thee, saith the LORD, to deliver thee.

Jeremiah 1:19

136

✦

God can't allow Himself to be tripped up.

And no man was able to answer him a word, neither durst any man from that day forth ask him any more questions.

Matthew 22:46

137

✳

God's forgiveness can't be calculated.

Then came Peter to him, and said, Lord, how oft shall my brother sin against me, and I forgive him? Till seven times? Jesus saith unto him, I say not unto thee, Until seven times: but, Until seventy times seven.

Matthew 18:21–22

138

✳

God can't leave you unfulfilled.

Blessed are they which do hunger and thirst after righteousness: for they shall be filled.

Matthew 5:6

139

God can't be
defined.

And God said unto Moses, I Am That
I Am.

Exodus 3:14

140

* * *

God can't allow His word to decay.

The grass withereth, and the flower thereof falleth away: But the word of the Lord endureth for ever.

I Peter 1:24–25

141

❖

God can't let you fight by yourself.

And all this assembly shall know that the LORD saveth not with sword and spear: for the battle is the LORD's, and he will give you into our hands.

I Samuel 17:47

142

*

God can't betray your trust.

And they that know thy name will put their trust in thee: for thou, LORD, hast not forsaken them that seek thee.

Psalm 9:10

143

※

God can't break a promise.

My covenant will I not break, nor alter
the thing that is gone out of my lips.

Psalm 89:34

144

❦

God can't ever allow His love to fail.

Charity never faileth: but whether there be prophecies, they shall fail; whether there be tongues, they shall cease; whether there be knowledge, it shall vanish away...And now abideth faith, hope, charity, these three; but the greatest of these is charity.

I Corinthians 13:8, 13

145

❋

God's word can't pass away.

Heaven and earth shall pass away, but
my words shall not pass away.

Matthew 24:35

146

✳

God can't leave you without final instructions.

Go ye therefore, and teach all nations, baptizing them in the name of the Father, and of the Son, and of the Holy Ghost: Teaching them to observe all things whatsoever I have commanded you: and, lo, I am with you always, even unto the end of the world. Amen.

Matthew 28:19–20

147

---❀---

God can't be given a problem He can't solve.

But Jesus beheld them, and said unto them, With men this is impossible; but with God all things are possible.

Matthew 19:26

148

✳

God can't have a bad plan for your life.

For I know the thoughts that I think toward you, saith the LORD, thoughts of peace, and not of evil, to give you an expected end.

Jeremiah 29:11

149

✳

God can't be surprised.

But he knoweth the way that I take: when he hath tried me, I shall come forth as gold.

Job 23:10

150

✳

God can't be selfish.

He that spared not his own Son, but
delivered him up for us all, how shall
he not with him also freely give us all
things?

Romans 8:32

151

God can't fail.

Be strong and of a good courage, fear not, nor be afraid of them: for the Lord thy God, he it is that doth go with thee; he will not fail thee, nor forsake thee.

Deuteronomy 31:6